Vanity &
Meaning

Discovering Purpose in Life

Edited by
R. C. Sproul Jr.

Ligonier
Ministries

Baker Books

A Division of Baker Book House Co
Grand Rapids, Michigan 49516

Published by Baker Books
a division of Baker Book House Company
P.O. Box 6287, Grand Rapids, MI 49516-6287

Printed in the United States of America

Library of Congress Cataloging-in-Publication Data

Sproul, R. C. Jr.
 Vanity and meaning : discovering purpose in life / R. C. Sproul Jr.,
 editor.
     p.   cm.
 ISBN 0-8010-5242-4 (paper)
 1. Bible. O.T. Ecclesiastes—Meditations. 2. Meaning (Philosophy)—
Biblical teaching. I. Sproul, R. C. (Robert Charles), 1939–   .
BS1475.4V36   1995
223'.806—dc20   95-674

The material contained in this book was originally published in *Tabletalk* magazine and was compiled in this format by the editor of *Tabletalk*, R. C. Sproul Jr.

Vanity &
Meaning

Also compiled from *Tabletalk*

Doubt and Assurance

Contents

Part 2   Good News
Life beyond the Sun Is Purposeful

Contributors

J. Kerby Anderson is an author and the host of the radio talk show *Newstalk*.

John H. Coe is assistant professor of philosophy and theology at Rosemead School of Psychology, Biola University, La Mirada, California.

Kyle Henderson is Ligonier Ministries' director of Internet communications.

Vinoy Laughner is managing editor of *Desktop Video World* in New Hampshire.

Mike Malone is pastor of St. Paul's Presbyterian Church (PCA) in Orlando, Florida.

Don Matzat, pastor of Messiah Lutheran Church in St. Louis, is the author of *Inner Healing: Deliverance or Deception, Christ Esteem,* and *Truly Transformed.* He hosts the daily radio broadcast *Issues, etc.*

John R. Muether is librarian and associate professor of bibliography and theological research at Reformed Theological Seminary, Orlando, Florida.

Ken Myers, former editor with National Public Radio, is host of the *Mars Hill Tapes,* an audiotape magazine on Christianity and culture.

R. C. Sproul is the John Dyer Trimble Professor of Systematic Theology at Reformed Theological Seminary,

Orlando, Florida, and chairman of Ligonier Ministries. Among his many books are *Before the Face of God, Book 2: A Guide for Living from the Old Testament*, and *Doubt and Assurance*.

R. C. Sproul Jr. is editor of *Tabletalk*, published by Ligonier Ministries, and author of *Dollar Signs of the Times*.

Mark R. Talbot is assistant professor of philosophy at Wheaton College, Wheaton, Illinois.

Donald S. Whitney, author of *Spiritual Disciplines for the Christian Life*, is pastor of Glenfield Baptist Church in Glen Ellyn, Illinois.

Part 1

Bad News

Life under the Sun Is Vanity

"In space no one can hear you scream." So intoned an ad for a popular horror movie. What was communicated was not so much the terror of the movie's monster but the more abject dread of the nothing. In space you're alone, isolated, cut off. Respond how you wish, because it doesn't matter. No one can hear you scream.

In the Book of Ecclesiastes the Teacher looks deep into the nothing. Like the lone soldier who survives a massacre and returns to recount the horror, the Teacher tells the ugly truth—unvarnished, unwashed. Under the sun is nothing but nothing. If nothing is what sleeping rocks dream of, I'm afraid they must be petrified with fear.

Perhaps the greatest horror of the nothing is the enticing mirages of something. As we explore the vast wasteland, suddenly our hearts sing, our energies become focused, and we pump our legs furiously to find the oasis of meaning. We dip our heads to drink, to satiate our burning thirst, only to taste the bitter sand scorched by an eternity under the sun.

In this first half of our study of vanity and meaning we will look at some of the mirages, the enticements under the sun through which the Teacher sought meaning. The Teacher chased wisdom, pleasure, riches. He sought meaning in his labor. The sum of the matter? The Teacher chased the wind.

The Teacher became a wise man at the end of his search. He had discovered an ancient truth when he declared, "There is nothing new under the sun" (1:9b). Those same mirages continue to lure us today. We too are fools, fooled by the lies of nothing. Nothing has changed—or rather, the nothing hasn't changed. It's still nothing and it's still trying to seduce us. Even believers, those "under the Son," sometimes hear the sirens sing.

However, we Christians are to live on a different plane. We are to live *coram Deo*, before the face of God. This is life not under but beyond the sun. There we find not nothing but the One Thing, the Somethingest Thing that could ever be, God himself. Living *coram Deo* means understanding that vanity is vain, futility futile, and chasing wind only so much chasing wind. With our hearts abiding beyond the sun, we care about those playing in the barren sands, those sinking into an eternal grave at Vanity Fair. Living *coram Deo* means sharing the warning of the Teacher that beneath the sun is only folly and beyond it only wisdom. It means drinking deep from the life-giving water of him who alone can satisfy our thirst.

1

Vanity of Vanities, All Is Vanity

R. C. Sproul

I have seen all the things that are done under the
sun; all of them are meaningless, a chasing after the
wind.

Ecclesiastes 1:14

"Vanity of vanities, all is vanity" (KJV). These words
begin the philosophically pregnant Book of Ecclesiastes. Their
literary structure forms an expression of the superlative
degree. Just as the New Testament expression "King of kings"
or "Lord of lords" indicates a supreme, or ultimate, king or
lord, so the vanity that is the vanity of vanities refers to a
supreme, or ultimate, vanity.

What is vanity? I know at least three distinct usages of this word. The first meaning I learned was in reference to a piece of furniture in my grandmother's bedroom, a kind of desk with a large mirror before which she sat to apply her makeup. The second usage I learned in junior high school. The school principal entered the men's room and observed me taking great pains to comb my hair properly. He warned me against vanity—a synonym for narcissistic pride or egotism, the kind of attitude Jimmy Connors says compels him to use the proper deodorant.

However, the vanity of which Ecclesiastes speaks is a matter far deeper. It is the vanity of meaninglessness, the vanity of futility. It captures the essence of a philosophical position called nihilism. To say "all is vanity" is to say that *nothing* has meaning or significance ultimately. Nihilism means literally "nothing-ism." The *nihil* corresponds to what Nietzsche called *das nichtig* (the nothing).

> *To say "all is vanity" is to say that* nothing *has meaning or significance ultimately.*

Nihilism has two traditional enemies—theism and naive humanism. The theist contradicts the nihilist because the existence of God guarantees the ultimate meaning and significance of personal life and history. The nihilist considers naive humanism naive because it rhapsodizes—with no rational foundation—the dignity and significance of human life. The humanist declares that humankind is a cosmic accident whose origin was fortuitous and whose destiny is annihilation. The two poles of human existence—origin and destiny—are both entrenched in meaningless insignificance. Yet between those poles the humanist mindlessly crusades for, defends, and celebrates the chimera of human dignity.

Philosophers like Jean-Paul Sartre and Albert Camus saw
the glaring Pollyannaish naiveté of such forms of humanism.
For Camus, the only serious question left for the philosopher
was the question of suicide. Sartre punctuated his literary
career with a little volume titled *Nausea*, in which he concluded that humankind is a "useless passion."

It is one thing to be useless. It is quite another to have feelings about it. When we discard something, we declare it useless. Now if the discarded object is a scrap of metal, we do not
risk hurting its feelings. A metal scrap has no passion. It does
not care about its destiny. It is mindless and feelingless.

However, if we discard a living human being, if we declare
a person useless, then we are dealing with real passion. Twen-
tieth-century existential philosophy has been almost preoccu-
pied with the concept of *Besörgen*. This refers to "care." Human
beings are caring creatures. They have feelings and passions.
They care because what happens in their lives matters to them.

Here is the dilemma: Nihilism declares that nothing really
matters ultimately. It may matter to us. But that does not
mean that it matters ultimately. We may care but the blind
forces of the universe do not care. They do not care at all.

To be in an environment of ultimate uncaring is the worst
fate that can befall a caring creature. It is to be sentenced to
a life of ultimate futility. Perhaps the naming of a mirrored
table as a vanity suggests that any effort to disguise our lack
of beauty with cosmetics is an exercise in futility. It is a cover-
up of the real—an illusion designed to camouflage the truth.

In the arena of logic there is a common informal fallacy
called the "false dilemma." It occurs when we simplistically
reduce all options to two when in fact there are many more.
Because of the pervasive use of this fallacy we tread on dangerous ground when we attempt such reductions. There are
times, however, when the peril must be ignored and the stance

taken. There are some issues that do resolve to either-or status. For example, either God exists or he does not. There is no *tertium quid*, no intermediate possibility.

When we ask the question of ultimate meaning, we have a similar either-or option. Either human life matters ultimately, or it does not. If it does not, then the conclusion cannot be resisted: "Vanity of vanities, all is vanity."

The author of Ecclesiastes is not wrestling with shadows or dealing with trifles. He is probing the ultimate question of human life, human passion, human aspiration, human caring—the question of meaning and significance. He knows that the question of ultimate meaning is a theological question. He understands that the question of ultimate meaning is linked inexorably to the question of ultimate being.

> *Either human life matters ultimately or it does not. If it does not, then the following conclusion cannot be resisted: "Vanity of vanities, all is vanity."*

First as a student and then as a professor of philosophy, I have long been convinced that ultimately there are only two serious philosophical options open to theoretical thought: nihilism and full-orbed theism. Between these polar opposites, I realize, resides an almost limitless number of variant philosophical schools. But the iron hand of logic forces all the hybrids to resolve to one or the other. All other systems are parasites. They live off the capital borrowed either from theism or nihilism. They suffer the gourmet's paradox: You cannot have your cake and eat it too.

In my judgment, no philosophical treatise has ever surpassed or equaled the penetrating analysis of the ultimate question of meaning versus vanity as that found in Ecclesiastes.

2

Wisdom under the Sun

J. Kerby Anderson

> Wisdom, like an inheritance, is a good thing and benefits those who see the sun. Wisdom is a shelter as money is a shelter, but the advantage of knowledge is this: that wisdom preserves the life of its possessor.
>
> Ecclesiastes 7:11–12

Does wisdom and its diligent pursuit bring happiness or sorrow? It all depends. Proverbs teaches that "blessed is the man who finds wisdom, the man who gains understanding" (3:13). However, in Ecclesiastes 1:18, the Teacher concludes, "For with much wisdom comes much sorrow; the more knowledge, the more grief."

Why the difference? In the first case the man who finds wisdom receives it from God. Earlier in Proverbs the writer teaches that true wisdom is based on "the fear of the LORD" (1:7). When our worldview is centered in the Lord and on an understanding of him, we will find true wisdom and happiness.

But what of other forms of wisdom? The Teacher says that seeking wisdom "under the sun" and the study of "all that is done under heaven" is "meaningless, a chasing after the wind" (Eccles. 1:3, 13–14). Basing our lives on the wisdom of the world is folly; our lives will be a vain and futile struggle for existence.

Knowledge alone does not bring wisdom. On the contrary, the Teacher notes that knowledge alone brings sorrow. Those who pursue wisdom under the sun, apart from God's revelation, will be disappointed and find it as effective as chasing after the wind.

Not only is this the testimony of Ecclesiastes, but it's the testimony of positivism over the last few centuries. French philosopher Auguste Comte set forth the proposition that all knowledge regarding matters of fact is based upon the "positive" data of experience. Only statements that can be verified through the senses have meaning. All other statements—for instance, "God exists" or "murder is wrong"—are not only false but meaningless. Comte, of course, did not find this thesis in a test tube and so refuted himself.

Best known for developing the modern discipline of sociology, Comte could be called the high priest and chief promoter of what he termed the "Religion of Humanity." He and his followers developed a priestly class, sacraments, and a catechism for this new religion of positivism, which spread throughout Europe.

Science, positivists argue, shows us that there is no need for supernatural explanations. Humankind, by studying nature and society, can formulate explanations of natural phenomena. Society can throw off all the mysticism of the past that attempted to explain the world in theological or metaphysical terms. Questions concerning ultimate reality or first causes are unimportant and of little interest since they are unanswerable.

As a speaker on campuses throughout North America, I have seen the devastating impact of positivism on our colleges and universities. Faculty members long ago abandoned the search for ultimate truth. They despair of finding any meaning in their academic pursuits—and even in their own lives.

Recently a friend of mine, working on a doctoral dissertation on postmodern thought, received a call from one of his professors. After briefly discussing the student's thesis, the professor began to pour out to the student the pain and despair in his life. He saw the futility of finding wisdom under the sun and despaired of finding any meaning in his academic studies or personal life. Then, even more surprisingly, this Nietzsche scholar asked the student for his prayers.

Students would agree with the Teacher's assessment in Ecclesiastes. There is no wisdom under the sun—only facts and observation. Students are drowning in a sea of meaningless data.

Students also feel this despair but in different ways. They know lots of information about the world, but they can rarely attach any meaning to it. Students can rattle off data, but they cannot put the facts together in any meaningful way because they do not have an epistemological framework to connect the facts.

Their problem is akin to the challenge facing a jigsaw puzzle aficionado. Putting the pieces together is easier if one has a box top picturing the finished puzzle. Each piece is easier to put into its proper place when one sees how it fits into the grand design.

In earlier centuries college students had a grand design to give meaning to all the facts. Even the word *university* (from *uni*, meaning one, and *veritas*, meaning truth) testified to this unified design. As secularism spread through the university, a humanistic worldview replaced a Christian one. Students found themselves in a predicament. They were like a person trying to put a jigsaw puzzle together while following the picture on the wrong box top. Some of the pieces fit, but the box top was more hindrance than help. By the time positivism spread through the university, students threw out the idea of a box top. Because there was no grand design, ultimate knowledge and wisdom were impossible.

> *Seeking wisdom under the sun rather than finding wisdom based on the fear of the Lord is folly.*

Students would agree with the Teacher's assessment in Ecclesiastes. There is no wisdom under the sun—only facts and observation. Students are drowning in a sea of meaningless data. They despair of finding any grand design, or *universitas*.

As positivist ideas have spread from campus to community, despair and meaninglessness have followed. Just as professor and student despair of finding truth and meaning, so does the average citizen. Seeking wisdom under the sun has become vanity and chasing after the wind. The cynicism and skepticism in the arts, politics, commerce, and the media all testify to the futility of trying to find wisdom and meaning in a world without God. The Teacher's words of old are still fitting. Seeking wisdom under the sun rather than finding wisdom based on the fear of the Lord is folly.

3

Too Much Pleasure

Kyle Henderson

> I denied myself nothing my eyes desired; I refused
> my heart no pleasure. My heart took delight in all my
> work, and this was the reward for all my labor. Yet when
> I surveyed all that my hands had done and what I had
> toiled to achieve, everything was meaningless, a chasing
> after the wind; nothing was gained under the sun.
>
> Ecclesiastes 2:10–11

"What in the world is that?" I mumbled, shocked out
of my midafternoon slumber by a loud crash in the hotel hallway. I stumbled out of bed and struggled with a pair of pants.
Without caution I flung open the door and peered down the
hall. A bizarre sight chased away all remaining sleepiness.

At the end of the hall stood a large naked man. With his bare fist he smashed a glass globe above a hotel-room door, shouting at the top of his lungs, "Too much power!"

I stood in the doorway stunned, speechless. Then he turned and saw me. "Too much power!" he bellowed again and ran straight for me.

The next few seconds defy clear recollection. Somehow I managed to run into my room, latch the door, and dive under the bed. My heart thumped as loudly as his footsteps as he approached the door. But he didn't stop at my room. He kept running, shouting again and again, "Too much power!" There was a huge crash of glass. The running stopped.

> *Pleasure is good. God made a good world, and he made us capable of delighting in our sensations of it. But the blessing of pleasure quickly becomes a curse when idolized.*

After a time I gingerly tiptoed to the door, straining my ears to detect even the slightest sound. All was quiet.

I opened the door—carefully this time. Nobody was in sight. The window at the end of the hallway was smashed; shards of glass jutted from the window frame.

The man had jumped through the second-story window.

I put on my shoes and walked to the end of the hall. There in the parking lot, in a growing pool of blood, the man stood. His back faced the hotel. His hands were folded in front of him. His head was bowed low. Now he appeared as he truly was—naked, ashamed, and completely powerless.

Mercifully, an ambulance arrived. Later I learned that he had taken PCP, a hallucinogenic drug. People under the influence of PCP often have almost superhuman strength—and equally strong delusions.

The man probably didn't know it, but he was a hedonist. Enslaved by a fervid desire for gratification, he used his mind not to inform his desires but to serve them. Objective truths, such as the laws of logic, became mere tools enabling him to conceive and implement strategies for obtaining and ingesting a powerful horse tranquilizer. The objective paid homage to the subjective. Principle deferred to passion. The flesh was willing and the spirit was weak.

The man got what he wanted. In fact, he got a little too much. That extra dose of pleasure, that extra stimulus to his brain, literally drove him out of his mind. Too much pleasure gave him too much power, bringing him nothing but pain.

Believe it or not, the Teacher in Ecclesiastes experienced something similar: "I denied myself nothing my eyes desired; I refused my heart no pleasure. My heart took delight in all my work" (2:10).

And what was the Teacher's conclusion? "Yet when I surveyed all that my hands had done and what I had toiled to achieve, everything was meaningless, a chasing after the wind; nothing was gained under the sun" (v. 11).

Pleasure is good. God made a good world, and he made us capable of delighting in our sensations of it. But the blessing of pleasure quickly becomes a curse when idolized. And that's exactly what has happened in our culture.

Over 1.5 million abortions take place in America annually, yet the horrible practice remains legal. Why? Because people value their desire for sexual pleasure more than they value the lives of unborn children. That's hedonism.

Our national and personal debt is profligate. Why? Because people value the pleasures of things, style, and government gifts more than they value old-fashioned disciplines such as saving for the future, personal responsibility, and freedom. That's hedonism.

And, worst of all, the church hasn't gone unscathed. Literature promoting the inanities of health-and-wealth charlatans, the therapies of pop "psychologians," and the sentimentalities of much modern "worship" is often far more popular than informative, enlivening works on orthodoxy and orthopraxy. Why? Because we often value the pursuit of personal fulfillment more than we value the quest for God. That's hedonism. And God deserves better from his children.

The Teacher found hedonism unprofitable. The pleasures that looked so attractive turned out to be fleeting and unsatisfying—doubly vain. Under the sun, true pleasure is impossible. But relativized by truth, pleasure has its proper place and leads to its proper end: God, at whose right hand are pleasures forevermore.

4

The Vanity of Riches

John R. Muether

> Whoever loves money never has money enough; who-
> ever loves wealth is never satisfied with his income. This
> too is meaningless. As goods increase, so do those who
> consume them. And what benefit are they to the owner
> except to feast his eyes on them?
>
> Ecclesiastes 5:10–11

When we study the Bible's teaching on wealth, we find
a curious ambivalence. On the one hand, there are several
passages that portray it positively. Abraham was "very wealthy
in livestock and in silver and gold" (Gen. 13:2). Job was a man
of great wealth, and Solomon was granted riches and honor

unparalleled in his day (1 Kings 3:13). Proverbs tells us that "the blessing of the LORD brings wealth" (10:22).

On the other hand, when the Teacher in Ecclesiastes described the meaninglessness of riches, he joined a chorus of biblical voices condemning wealth. In the parable of the rich young man, Jesus showed the folly of being materially rich but poor in one's relationship with God. It is difficult for the rich to come to faith, he said. The poor have a better sense of the futility of their own resources, and for this reason Christ blessed the poor.

This witness concerning money is not a contradiction. It can be harmonized when we understand that the Bible condemns false attitudes toward wealth. It is not wealth itself that is condemned but greed and envy; the *love of* money is the root of all sorts of evil. In Augustine's distinction God alone is to be enjoyed *(fruitio)*, and all else is to be used *(usus)* in order to attain what can be enjoyed. Idolatry results when this formula is reversed, when we seek to enjoy those things that cannot produce true joy and satisfaction.

> *It is not wealth itself that is condemned but greed and envy; the* love *of money is the root of all sorts of evil.*

And how often we do reverse that formula. Envy is the earliest and most pervasive vice in the biblical narrative. Because of the envy of Satan the fall took place. Envy was the cause of the first murder. The Philistines envied Isaac (Gen. 26:14). Rachel envied her sister (Gen. 30:1). Joseph's brothers envied him (Gen. 37:11). Envy's deadly effect is recorded in Job: "Resentment kills a fool, and envy slays the simple" (5:2). Proverbs says that envy rots the bones (14:30), and the Psalms too counsel against it. The apostle Paul labels greed a form of idolatry (Eph. 5:5), as it demands allegiance which is due God alone.

Jesus said: "Watch out! Be on your guard against all kinds of greed" (Luke 12:15). Paul noted that greed would be particularly prevalent in the last days (2 Tim. 3:1ff.). For us to be faithful to Jesus' warning, not only must we see envy as a perennial problem, we ought also to understand the particular ways in which it manifests itself in our age.

Contemporary discussions of economic justice often focus on greed as the province of the wealthy. We think of the capitalist robber barons of the late nineteenth century or the insider traders of the 1980s. "Greed is good!" thundered Michael Douglas in the film *Wall Street*. Yet much of our criticism of greed is itself a manifestation of a covetous attitude that festers among the deprived as much as the endowed. (This has been aptly called "the politics of envy.") Not only does greed plague all classes in our culture, it finds expression in the self-centeredness of a consumerist mentality that puts a monetary value on all of life.

A recent article in *The New Republic* lamented the "tyranny of choice," describing how consumerism is inducing us to expand our appetites in unhealthy ways. The ubiquity of choice, and its temptations toward greed, extends far beyond the disease of credit-card debt, eroding any sense of contentment and commitment. The insistence that we constantly upgrade our cars and computers and CD players spills over into more important commitments—the family, work, and the church.

In our search for the perfect marriage we often experience struggles in marital relationships. Less and less do we seek to solve them through slow and often painful processes. Instead we opt for more convenient alternatives. As a result, divorce rates are sky-high.

Moreover, we have even created mechanisms for children to divorce their parents! Television celebrity Rosanne Arnold recently announced that she was removing her parents from her life. From now on she would live as if they had fallen off a cliff. "After all," she argued, "you don't choose your parents." Consider the irony of her logic. The expression "You don't choose your relatives" has usually been understood to mean that, for good or ill, you are stuck with your family. But Arnold, bowing to the idol of choice, draws the opposite conclusion: She is free from her family precisely because she *didn't* choose them.

Abortion is another way consumerism attacks the family. Proabortion forces carefully couch their rhetoric in the language of choice. This is particularly effective because it capitalizes on our greedy insistence on personal autonomy. Who wants to go on record against choice?

Not only does greed plague all classes in our culture, it finds expression in the self-centeredness of a consumerist mentality that puts a monetary value on all of life.

Robert Bellah and his associates in the book *Habits of the Heart* noted how a greedy individualism affects the way in which we view work, as the traditional idea of a calling has been replaced by the modern idea of a career. *Calling* suggests a specific function within a community. *Career*, on the other hand, is an expression of a personal agenda, a course of life that is designed to maximize personal happiness. The goal is no longer service to others but the achievement of success.

Likewise, in the church, if we are uncomfortable with our church's youth program or its "worship style," we need not be troubled. We can simply check out an alternative down the street. Gone is the slow path of discipleship and submission in order to mature in the unity of the faith. In its place is this demand: What about my needs? Pastors are told to accommodate to this consumeristic impulse if they expect their churches to grow.

Greed, then, takes on subtle forms in modern life. Modernity, sociologists tell us, is about the destruction of traditional orders. Greed, in both its classical and contemporary expressions, is about the destruction of God's created order. Like Satan, the first to envy, we refuse our God-ordained place in creation. Priding ourselves in our detachment from the past, we declare ourselves free, Gatsby-like, to reinvent ourselves, to design our own identities. And we re-create our social structures—family, work, and church—to meet our personal cravings.

The new "order" that we create is a deadening disorder. Our search for the perfect marriage, job, or church can never meet our inflated, ego-driven expectations. It is futile because, as Augustine showed, it substitutes the love of things for the love of God. We become enslaved to the idol of consumerism. "This too is vanity."

5

Thou Art the Man

R. C. Sproul Jr.

> What does a man get for all the toil and anxious striving with which he labors under the sun? All his days his work is pain and grief; even at night his mind does not rest. This too is meaningless.
>
> Ecclesiastes 2:22–23

It was a budget tour, a whirlwind trip. Such things should be expected. I was seeing Europe with the speed of the Nazi blitzkrieg, crossing borders on a bus. It was old-fashioned American capitalism at work, culture for sale at bargain-basement prices. Our hurried movement from museum to museum, from fashion Mecca to fashion Mecca, would leave me a sophisticated *bon vivant* in three short weeks.

At seventeen I was a Philistine, both in terms of fashion and the arts. I knew enough, however, to look forward to our times in the museums more than in the shopping bazaars. Let me die in sartorial ignorance, but let me learn to appreciate beauty.

More than any other, one great work demanded my attention. I found the *Mona Lisa* less than enticing. Rembrandt held no appeal. I yawned at the canals of Venice. I turned up my nose at the Sistine Chapel. But I counted down the days and miles until we would reach Florence. I wanted to see Michelangelo's *David*.

Our bus pulled into Florence as the sun was setting. It pulled out the next morning as the sun was rising. Between our arrival and departure the museum was closed. I left without seeing the *David*.

A crowd had gathered in the bus around Randy, a fellow traveler. I listened in, green with envy as he told of his early morning adventure. Somehow he had gotten into the museum and stolen a private audience with the *David*. For five minutes he had beheld the majestic statue in silence, undisturbed by crowds and flashing cameras. For a brief moment he had stopped being a tourist doing his duty and had become a man appreciating Man. Only the frantic shouts and gestures of the guards had forced him out of his reverie. And I had missed it.

Randy had seen all that I had wanted to see. David, the man, was all that I wanted to be. He was strong, brave, confident, heroic. Michelangelo captured all that in stone. He was the ultimate multitalented Renaissance man.

Michelangelo was devout. His devotion, however, was to his gift, not to its Giver. He appropriated the biblical ideal of David and sculpted the Renaissance ideal: man as man, the greatest being imaginable. He had taken David's strength, bravery, confidence, and heroism and carved them in stone.

But he left out the context. Using a man who created psalms, odes to God, Michelangelo created an ode to vanity.

The glory of David is not the vibrancy of youthful promise, not the lean and taut muscles, not the self-assured glance of the statue. Rather, the glory is that David was a man after God's own heart. Michelangelo gave David a heart of stone. God gave him a heart of flesh. All the beauty, all the conquest, all the talents—all are vanity in themselves. Without the heart that beats beyond the sun, art, life, and humankind are pure folly.

David is the man, an Old Testament ideal. He pointed both backward to Adam and forward to Christ. His rule was the golden age of Israel. He was an artist, creating the songs for a nation. He was a king and the father of kings. He walked with God.

He was also an adulterer and a murderer. Such a discordant note breaks the glorious harmony. How prophetic were the words of the prophet Nathan: "Thou art the man."

And David is us. We were kings, created by the King: "[You] crowned him with glory and honor" (Ps. 8:5b). We were given rule in a true golden age: "You made him ruler over the works of your hands; you put everything under his feet" (Ps. 8:6). We were artists, tending to a beautiful garden. God came and spoke with us in the cool of the evening.

Without the heart that beats beyond the sun, art, life, and humankind are pure folly.

We too became adulterers and murderers. We became lost in vanity. The image of God in us became shattered by sin. It is the character of God, his imperial majesty and righteousness, that stands before us like Nathan—pointing, accusing, judging rightly. It is of that character that David sings throughout the Psalms. He neither hides from it nor cringes at it but rejoices in the God of his salvation. The Psalms always remind us of God's greatness and our dependence upon him. They leave no room for self-aggrandizement.

> *The character of God, his imperial majesty and righteousness, stands before us like Nathan — pointing, accusing, judging rightly.*

We should continually recall the vanity of life beneath the sun and keep ever in mind the folly of all our labor. Let Nathan accuse us of our wickedness. And then let us repent.

Let not our former created majesty be a cause of self-glory. Let us never forget our context and thank ourselves for the gifts God has given. Let us build no monument, no David-like sculpture, to proclaim our dignity, nor lift the head of Goliath, the conquered foe, as a triumphant sacrifice.

If we are like David, men and women after God's own heart, we will bring the sacrifice of David. We will respond to God's holiness as David responded after Nathan's judgment: "You do not delight in sacrifice, or I would bring it; you do not take pleasure in burnt offerings. The sacrifices of God are a broken spirit; a broken and contrite heart, O God, you will not despise" (Ps. 51:16–17).

6

Toiling the Soul

Don Matzat

Whatever exists has already been named, and what
man is has been known; no man can contend with one
who is stronger than he. The more the words, the less
the meaning, and how does that profit anyone?

Ecclesiastes 6:10–11

Counselors and therapists, utilizing the techniques of
modern psychology, toil to improve the quality of life by pro-
ducing more responsible, better-adjusted human beings. This
is certainly a noble and lofty goal. Perhaps we should thank
God for such people who have worked to heal emotional
wounds, restore homes and families, and produce functional
people.

However, given the biblical teaching on the total deprav-
ity of humankind, and given that God has turned this world
over to all sorts of perverted behavior (Rom. 1:24, 26, 28),
one wonders just how effective this noble effort will be. We
do well to heed the Teacher in Ecclesiastes: "What does a man
get for all the toil and anxious striving with which he labors
under the sun? All his days his work is pain and grief; even
at night his mind does not rest. This too is meaningless"
(2:22–23).

Self-Esteem

To accomplish the noble goal of adjusting human behavior, theories concerning why and wherefore must be proposed.
Until recently, behaviorism and Freudianism were the two
main schools. Both viewpoints reduced human beings to creatures whose behavior was influenced or determined by outside
forces.

The "third force," or humanist psychology, arrived in the
late '50s and early '60s. Led by Carl Rogers, Erich Fromm,
and Abraham Maslow, the humanists
desired to return to human beings the
power over their own lives. They taught
that humans are conscious, responsible beings, able to take control over
their own lives, behavior, and emotions.
Out of the humanist school came the
notion that developing self-esteem and
striving to maintain a positive self-
image will deeply and positively affect
behavior, emotions, and productivity.

> *The message of
> Scripture is clear:
> The human
> dilemma is
> caused by human
> sinful nature.*

According to the self-esteem advocates, our behavioral and
emotional problems are the result of a negative self-image cre-

ated by those who have influenced our lives. Our parents did us a grave disservice by calling us "bad boys and girls," though our behavior warranted the label. When we flunked a test, our teachers made us feel stupid by criticizing us. And the Christian church, a major culprit, stirred within us deep guilt feelings by referring to us as poor, miserable sinners.

After thirty years of self-esteem, have we become a kinder, wiser, and gentler society? Hardly.

Victimization and Abuse

Within recent years there has been a shift in the popular self-help themes. The buzzwords of *self-esteem* and *positive self-image* have been replaced with *victimization, abuse,* and *multiple personality disorder.* The present craze among counselors and therapists is to go beyond the superficial search for self-esteem and uncover the deep wounds and emotional scars in their clients' past that lie at the roots of their aberrant behavior and emotional malaise.

It's Not My Fault

Given the checkered track record of psychological counseling and therapy, why does it remain a multimillion-dollar business?

All of the cause-and-effect theories of human behavior proposed by psychology have one thing in common: They appeal to the most basic human need to avoid responsibility or accepting blame. Adam said, "It's not my fault. It's that woman you gave me." The French philosopher Blaise Pascal believed that the natural human desire to preserve oneself and refuse to accept blame is as strong as the desire for food and shelter.

The Proper Perspective

In the seventh chapter of Romans the apostle Paul deals with the human dilemma. The good he wants to do, Paul writes, he doesn't do. The evil he wants to refrain from doing, he finds himself doing. Sound typical? The problem is no great mystery. It is sin. Paul concludes that he is powerless to change his life, because sin dwells within. He cries out in despair, "What a wretched man I am!" The message of Scripture is clear: The human dilemma is caused by human sinful nature.

God does have the solution to the human dilemma. It does not involve adjusting something within the human psyche. Rather, God desires to add something new to the sinner—the forgiveness of sins, the righteousness and life of the person of his Son, Jesus Christ. God simply instructs us in his Word to get off ourselves and live in the benefits that belong to us in Christ Jesus.

Receiving the divine solution demands the acceptance of the divine diagnosis. Arriving at the conclusion that "I am the problem and Jesus is the solution" opens a storehouse of life-changing spiritual benefits.

7

Fear God and Obey

Mike Malone

Much dreaming and many words are meaningless.
Therefore stand in awe of God.

Ecclesiastes 5:7

This is the Age of Information. If the amount of available knowledge accumulated from the beginning of recorded history until 1900 is considered one unit, we possessed three units by 1950. Those three units quadrupled in the next forty years.

The amount of information that confronts us has produced an attendant assumption: Because there is more to know, it is good to know more.

Ecclesiastes stands in stark contrast to the modern world at precisely this point. The opening chapters describe the futility of knowing for the sake of knowing. The terms *wisdom* and *knowledge* are used frequently in this book. Generally speaking, knowledge refers to what may be known—in other words, information. But wisdom is different. Wisdom is information rightly considered and rightly applied. A person may know a great deal about atomic energy yet apply his knowledge unwisely. Knowledge is raw information, brute facts. Nothing, however, is "known" as a brute fact. Whatever is known is known by someone. And when it is known, it immediately becomes either foolishness or wisdom. There is no foolish information. But there are many fools.

What have we gained with all our information? Are we better off? Is the acquisition of knowledge, apart from the consideration of God, necessarily a good thing? This century has excelled in the acquisition and proliferation of knowledge, but Sarajevo, Mogadishu, Beirut, Berlin, Ulster, Bogota, and countless other cities are a ringing testimony to our failure to apply rightly what we know. So much looks so futile, so vain, so empty when South Central Los Angeles burns, feudal warlords plunder a desperate people in a desperate land, and monotheists of varying stripes butcher one another in the wake of the dissolution of the Soviet Union.

> *"Fear God and keep his commandments, for this is the whole duty of man."*

The Teacher in Ecclesiastes laments such suffering and cruelty: "I saw the tears of the oppressed—and they have no comforter; power was on the side of their oppressors—and they have no comforter. And I declared that the dead, who had already died, are happier than the living, who are still alive. But better than both is he who has not yet been, who has not seen the evil that is done under the sun" (4:1b–3). Knowing for the sake of knowing doesn't seem to be the answer.

Knowledge should lead to wisdom. After years of inquiry and thoughtfulness, the writer of Ecclesiastes draws conclusions. He is not forever accumulating more information. He is not forever investigating the latest technology, the most current theory. He grows weary of the machinations of mere humans.

The Teacher concludes: "Of making many books there is no end, and much study wearies the body. Now all has been heard; here is the conclusion of the matter: Fear God and keep his commandments, for this is the whole duty of man" (Eccles. 12:12b–13). This is no deprecation of the intellect. Indeed, the Teacher has found an object of inquiry that will tax all of his resources to the limit. He asserts that not all knowledge has equal value. Some things are more worth knowing than others. To be wise means to be discriminating. It means differentiating things of eternal value from those with only temporary significance. Knowing God is the highest possible knowledge. It is knowledge calculated to thrill the soul and satisfy the deepest longings of the human heart. It is knowledge so high and lofty that it transcends language, which can never exhaust the glorious reality of God.

The wise man would take us by the hand and lead us to the fountain of God's wisdom, where we may drink to our heart's content—where we will never imbibe enough, yet never fail to be satisfied.

8

And Then We Die?

Ken Myers

> All go to the same place; all come from dust, and to dust all return. Who knows if the spirit of man rises upward and if the spirit of the animal goes down into the earth?
>
> Ecclesiastes 3:20–21

In the 1960s Swedish film director Ingmar Bergman made three films that dealt with the themes of emptiness, alienation, boredom, and the difficulty of relationships in the absence of transcendental values. These were not new themes in Bergman's work, but they were intensified in *Through a Glass Darkly, Winter Light,* and *The Silence.*

Thanks to Bergman's artistry, these popular modern themes were communicated with great power, in part because

Bergman refused to suggest answers to the Big Questions of life that he felt were finally unanswerable. He faced the tragic consequences of unbelief squarely, concluding (in the words of Arthur Gibson) that "man's quest for knowledge is, in truth, a bitter one, so much so that the twin horns of reason and impulse which he is condemned to ride do eventually impale him. Life itself is a dying-in."

The sensibility of many of Bergman's films suggests the tension experienced by those who perceive the vanity of a world without God, who perceive the reality of God (Rom. 1:19ff.), but who refuse to honor this reality in their thinking. Their profession of unfaith is a nagging, bitter profession, for at some level they recognize the merits of faith.

> *"Man's quest for knowledge is, in truth, a bitter one, so much so that the twin horns of reason and impulse which he is condemned to ride do eventually impale him. Life itself is a dying-in."*

The skepticism of Bergman and other modern artists was an uneasy skepticism. Close to the spirit of Ecclesiastes, the artists agonized over the alleged silence of God. But since the 1960s, in fiction, films, and other art forms, new moods have emerged that seem tailored to harden hearts much more ruthlessly.

While the modern spirit has replaced the truth of God with other sorts of truths, what some call the postmodern spirit defiantly and often gleefully rejects all substitutes for God. It lampoons any efforts to find an escape from the vanity of existence by erecting new gods—Reason, Science, the Self, the Artist, Progress.

Celebrating this vanity seems to be a trend in an emerging school of writers and thinkers who recognize that restlessness and cosmic homelessness are the natural state of humankind and therefore something to enjoy rather than lament.

In Milan Kundera's novel *The Unbearable Lightness of Being, lightness* signifies the same thing *silence* did in Bergman: the absence of transcendent values. But while many of the characters in the novel nostalgically long for weightedness, Sabina, one of the principal characters, happily embraces *lightness.* She is at home with homelessness. For her, and for an increasing number of our contemporaries, the absence of meaning, of rootedness, of a firm sense of self, is not a problem but an opportunity.

Mark Edmundson, commenting in *Harper's* magazine on Salman Rushdie's *The Satanic Verses,* concludes: "Homelessness, in this novel, is understood as humanity's condition—and one, finally, to be affirmed because it allows for more metamorphosis, change, the ability (and need) to be other than one was."

> *"Thou hast formed us for Thyself, and our hearts are restless till they find rest in Thee."*

There is a hint of that spirit in the work of a filmmaker who has honored (and parodied) Bergman in his work. Woody Allen also deals with the themes of boredom, alienation, and the deafening silence of God. But, as Allan Bloom perceptively notes, "Woody Allen helps to make us feel comfortable with nihilism, to Americanize it." Modern culture has come a long way from Bergman's *The Silence* to Woody Allen's "nihilism without the abyss."

This "Don't worry about the vanity of things, be happy" philosophy shows up in the recent book by psychologist Kenneth Gergen, *The Saturated Self.* Gergen argues that modern mobility has made us so rootless that we need to grow up and realize that the quest for meaning is a dangerous waste of time. "Many of our major problems in society result from taking seriously such terms as *reality, authenticity, true, worthwhile, superior, essential, valid, ideal, correct,* and the like." Gergen prescribes wholehearted assent to relativism as an antidote to agonizing over the vanity of existence. Stop complaining about the silence of God and the absence of truth. That's the way it is, so enjoy life.

For centuries the restlessness and sense of alienation that might be summarized as vanity have led men and women on a spiritual quest for something more. Augustine commenced his *Confessions* with this observation: "Thou hast formed us for Thyself, and our hearts are restless till they find rest in Thee."

But when the structures of modern life (including mobility, channel surfing, and frenetic video games) bless restlessness not as a condition to transcend but as the happy and normal state of things, the impediments to faith are significantly increased. Existential despair is now an old-fashioned response, closer to Augustine than to many modern novelists. At least Bergman sensed that the silence of God was a bitter tragedy. The more common sentiment today is to embrace vanity as (in the patois of Beavis and Butthead) "cool."

Part 2

Good News

Life beyond the Sun Is Purposeful

In a chapter of his book *Amusing Ourselves to Death*, Neil Postman focuses on how television news damages our ability to make connections. He reasons that television news purports to tell us those events that are significant, but does so in a disjointed manner. When the announcer declares, "And now this," we receive a signal to forget what we have just heard and to focus on what is coming. What we heard seconds before is now old news; what's coming is the new news.

Thus far we have looked at the vanity of life. We have explored how life "under the sun" is foolishness, devoid of meaning. And now this: we turn our attention to purpose, how life "beyond the sun" is replete with meaning and significance. What we have studied is the bad news; what's coming is the good news.

Unlike television news, however, there is a connection. The good news is the answer to the bad news. We have looked at the futility of wisdom, pleasure, riches, and labor under the sun. Now we peer beyond the sun and discover purpose in revelation, moderation, charity, and rest.

The rebuttal to the lament of the Teacher, "Vanity of vanities, all is vanity," is not "Purpose of purpose, *some* is purpose." *All* is purpose. The good news is not merely that portions of our lives have meaning but that every second has meaning. When we sleep through our lives—waiting and dreaming of some event, some beast in the jungle, that will one day arrive to give us significance—when we hold our breath in anticipation of our allotted fifteen minutes of fame, we misunderstand. When we see our lives as the evening news, in terms of screaming headlines, we fail to live *coram Deo*.

Living *coram Deo*, before the face of God, means living all our life to his glory. That does not mean just work, family, church, and leisure but *all* of work, *all* of family, *all* of church, and *all* of leisure. It means that the ordinary, the unspectacular, is imbued with significance. Living *coram Deo* is remembering that not a hair falls from one's head if our Father does not will it so. If he wills it, it has meaning. The proximate meaning may be shrouded, but we know that it has meaning ultimately because it gives him glory.

Living *coram Deo* means seeing the immanent in terms of the transcendent, the transient in terms of the eternal, the proximate in terms of the ultimate. It means remembering that right now counts forever.

And now this: *Gloria, in excelsis Deo.*

9

Vanity Overwhelmed by Purpose

R. C. Sproul

> Consider what God has done: Who can straighten what he has made crooked? When times are good, be happy; but when times are bad, consider: God has made the one as well as the other. Therefore, a man cannot discover anything about his future.
>
> Ecclesiastes 7:13–14

Why? This simple question, which we utter many times a day, is loaded with assumptions of what philosophers call *teleology*. Teleology is the study or science of purpose. The term comes from the Greek word *telos*, which is sprinkled liberally through the New Testament. The "why" questions are questions of purpose. We seek to discover the reason for things happening as they do. Why does the rain fall? Why does the earth turn on its axis? Why did you say what you said?

When we raise the question of purpose, we are concerned with ends, aims, and goals. All of these terms suggest intent. They assume meaning rather than meaninglessness.

In chapter 1 we considered the question of vanity. That which is vain is ultimately a-teleological; it lacks a definite purpose. It is the opposite of purpose.

The cynic may respond to the question Why? with the glib retort, Why not? Yet even in this response there is a thinly veiled commitment to purpose. If we give a reason for *not* doing something, we are saying that the negative serves a purpose or fulfills a goal. Human beings are creatures committed to purpose. Intent informs our actions.

Edmund Husserl defined the uniqueness of our humanity in terms of our capacity to act with "intentionality." That simply means that we do things for a reason—with a purpose in mind. The hunter aims his gun. The golfer lines up his putt. The business executive sets goals. The football player cuts toward the end zone.

In the quest for purpose we must distinguish between *proximate* and *remote* purposes. The proximate refers to that which is close at hand. The remote refers to the distant, ultimate purpose. The football player's proximate goal is to make a first down. The more remote goal is the touchdown. The even more remote goal is to win the game. The ultimate goal is to win the Super Bowl.

We remember the poignant meeting between Joseph and his brothers in which the brothers feared recriminations from their powerful brother for the treachery they had committed against him. But Joseph saw a remarkable concurrence at work between proximate and remote intentions. He said, "You meant it for evil; God meant it for good."

Here the proximate and the remote seemed to be mutually exclusive. The divine intention was the exact opposite of the human intention. Joseph's brothers had one goal; God had a different one. The amazing truth here is that the remote purpose was served by the proximate one. This does not diminish the culpability of the brothers. Their intent was evil and their actions were evil. Yet it seemed good to God to let it happen so that his purpose might be fulfilled.

With us there are accidents, indeed tragic accidents. Last fall our receptionist cut her fingers severely with an electric hedge clipper. She did not mean to cut her fingers. Her goal was to cut the bushes. In a proximate sense she had an accident. She may have asked, Why did God allow it to happen?

> *It is the good purpose of God that gives the final answer to the appearance of vanity and futility in this world. To trust in the good purpose of God is the very essence of godly faith.*

This question seeks to probe the remote or ultimate purpose. The question assumes something crucial to our understanding of God. It assumes that God *could have* prevented it. If we deny this verity we deny the very character of God. If God could *not* have prevented it, he would no longer really be God. By asking Why? we assume something else that is vital. We assume that there is an answer to the question. We assume that God had a *reason*, or a *purpose*, for what happened.

The question remains: Was God's reason or purpose a good one? To ask the question is to answer it if we know anything about God. We err in our reason. We establish futile goals. We rush off on fools' errands. We pursue sinful ends. Let us not project the same kind of vicious intentionality on God.

The only purpose or intention God ever has is altogether good. When the Bible speaks of the sovereign exercise of the pleasure of his will, there is no hint of arbitrariness or wicked intent. The pleasure of his will is always the *good* pleasure of his will. His pleasure is always good, his will is always good, his intentions are always good.

> *This is my Father's world and he rules it without caprice. As long as God exists, vanity is a manifest impossibility.*

When the apostle Paul declares the mysterious and breathtaking promise that "in all things God works for the good of those who love him, who have been called according to his purpose" (Rom. 8:28), he is musing on matters of teleology. He is dealing with the realm of the remote rather than the proximate. This insists that the proximate always be judged in the light of the remote.

Our problem is this: We do not yet possess the full light of the remote. We are still looking into a dark mirror. But we are not utterly devoid of light. We have enough light to know that God has a good purpose even when we are ignorant of that good purpose.

It is the good purpose of God that gives the final answer to the appearance of vanity and futility in this world. To trust in the good purpose of God is the very essence of godly faith. This is why no Christian can ultimately be a pessimist. The wicked aims of mice and men that surround and beset us daily may incline us toward pessimism—but only at the level of the proximate. I am not optimistic about human government or the innate good will of human beings. I am utterly optimistic about divine government and the intrinsic good will of God.

The world in which we live is not a world of chance. Its beginning was not an accident; its operation is not an accident; its *telos*, or goal, is not an accident. This is my Father's world and he rules it without caprice. As long as God exists, vanity is a manifest impossibility.

10

Revelation above and below the Sun

John H. Coe

Not only was the Teacher wise, but also he imparted knowledge to the people. He pondered and searched out and set in order many proverbs. The Teacher searched to find just the right words, and what he wrote was upright and true.

Ecclesiastes 12:9–10

As a Christian devoted to "the God who is there and who is not silent," I lament over two warring factions, each with half of the truth, each unable to resolve the conflict concerning the true nature of wisdom. On the one hand, I weep for modernity, which as a child of the Enlightenment wages war equipped with its dogmatic doctrine of all-sufficient wisdom "under the sun." In this view the light of human reason alone is sufficient for understanding nature, human nature, and what constitutes happiness. If there is a God, he does not reveal himself in word or person but only through the light of reason and science, which are his promises for a beautiful tomorrow.

As sad as modernity is, I take up another lamentation for the war-weary church, particularly those sections of evangelicalism that have reacted hastily to the repeated attacks from the Enlightenment philosophy. In their unguarded zeal to defend the Bible and its view of a God who reveals himself in word and person, they have adopted a Bible-centered reductionism of the Christian faith that focuses upon the sufficiency of Scripture at the expense of attending to the *fullness* of revelation. Thus, out of a defensive and reactive posture, they have retreated from the light of reason and natural revelation to the island of faith and cling desperately and unfortunately to an illusory Bible-alone approach to "wisdom that is solely from above."

Thomas Aquinas asserts with the history of theology that the infinite, personal God can be known not as he is in himself but only in his effects. Were it not for this self-chosen revelation, the knowledge of God would be the private and wonderful possession of the Godhead. But God condescended in eternity to speak powerfully in nature, word, and person.

Only when *all* forms of revelation are taken together can we speak of the sufficiency of revelation. Subtract one and we are left with a truncated view of both God and creation.

For instance, God revealed himself powerfully through the incarnation (John 1:14; Heb. 1:1–2), the indwelling Spirit (Rom. 8:14–17), and his mighty acts, the mightiest of which is the work of his Son. However, without the Scriptures or propositional revelation, these acts of God would be shrouded in haunting silence. The life and death of our Lord would have no meaning for us if God had not provided an interpretation through the mouth of Christ and the pens of the apostles. Even the work of the indwelling Spirit would take place in a meaningless vacuum. With holy events as mere symbols void of meaning, the church would be abandoned to theological agnosticism.

Propositional revelation, then, is especially significant to the Christian. As the inspired interpretation of the person and work of God, it opens up the possibility for salvation and re-creation. It also provides insight into life of which natural wisdom may be uncertain or ignorant.

However, propositional revelation alone is also inadequate insofar as it is incapable of saving a single soul. That is, the Christian faith does not affirm the sufficiency of Scripture per se, for only God can save on the basis of the finished work of Christ, as applied to the human heart in redemption through the Holy Spirit, by whom we know God as Father. Moreover, the Bible's intention is not to supplant the wisdom available from natural revelation but only to perfect that wisdom, bringing it to its *telos*, or goal, in Christ. Thus, the Bible provides the divine interpretation of aspects of history and nature. But alone it is insufficient.

> *Only when all forms of revelation are taken together can we speak of the sufficiency of revelation. Subtract one and we are left with a truncated view of both God and creation.*

Finally, natural revelation has been one of the more controversial and misunderstood forms of revelation recognized

by the church. In the creation God expresses his glory and
nature (Ps. 19:1–6), his goodness (Acts 17:24ff.), his justice and
wrath against sin (Rom. 1:18). This knowledge is not merely
the conclusion to an argument in natural theology, though
this may be the case as well. Rather, the psalmist and the apostle Paul refer to this knowledge of God as a correlate of human
consciousness—a knowledge as present to consciousness as, in
Calvin's words, the knowledge of oneself. However, this revelation is unique insofar as it is mediated nonproportionally
via creation and universally known by pagan and believer
alike—regardless of education, psychological makeup, or
attempts to suppress it.

Thus, before all other revelation, God spoke creation, his
first self-expression in space and time. This creation, in
Aquinas's words, reveals something of the nature of God much
in the way a painting reveals something of the painter. But
the divine Painter had no canvas. He painted *ex nihilo*. He had
no world or reality to represent except his own nature.

Consequently, when the natural and human sciences study
the natural laws governing creation, they study the nature of
God—at least in an analogical way, like the study of a painting
is a study of the painter. In this sense the sciences and common sense (when they speak truly) are ultimately expressions
of God's glory and wisdom, "promulgated" (to use Aquinas's
word) through creation.

Of course, natural revelation and wisdom alone do not save
people from their sin. Nature after the fall cannot redeem
itself. This is the damning mistake of the Enlightenment and
its liberal theological child, both trusting the voices of reason and science to usher in paradise. Instead, natural revelation condemns all people, exposes their guilt, and leaves them
in an inexcusable state of sin (Rom. 1:18–32). The Hebrew
sage acknowledges this and sets forth constraints for enthu-

siastic students of nature who might get carried away, incorrectly supposing that natural wisdom alone is ultimate and sufficient for happiness (see Ecclesiastes) or capable of successfully treating every human malady (see Job). Thus, the sage is conscious of the insufficiency of both the Bible alone and natural wisdom alone.

The Scriptures inform us that the war of either-or is a futile battle. We Christians can end this senseless skirmish by affirming the sufficiency of revelation in its fullness rather than merely in part. Only then are we equipped to enter the arena of ideas and contend for what we and the world need: the wisdom of God from above and below the sun.

11

Enjoying God's Gifts

Mark R. Talbot

> There is a time for everything, and a season for every
> activity under heaven.
>
> Ecclesiastes 3:1

One striking feature of Ecclesiastes is that while it condemns the life of pleasure-seeking as vain and meaningless, it
also commends accepting life's proper pleasures as gifts from
God: "It is good and proper for a man to eat and drink, and to
find satisfaction in his toilsome labor under the sun during the
few days of life God has given him—for this is his lot. Moreover,
when God gives any man wealth and possessions, and enables
him to enjoy them, to accept his lot and be happy in his work—
this is a gift of God" (5:18–19; see also 9:7–9).

For every reference in Ecclesiastes condemning excessive pleasure-seeking, there are two commending the legitimate enjoyment of life (see 8:15). The "heart of fools," the Teacher tells us, resides "in the house of pleasure" (7:4). But it is not, he thinks, the part of a wise person, who understands the place of human beings in God's scheme of things, to spurn life's proper pleasures when they come along.

The New Testament's attitude toward pleasure is much the same. The apostle Paul castigates those who are "lovers of pleasure rather than lovers of God" (2 Tim. 3:4). He declares that the widow who lives her life for pleasure is spiritually dead even while she is yet physically alive (1 Tim. 5:6). He also observes that, before salvation, we are all "foolish, disobedient, deceived and enslaved by all kinds of passions and pleasures" (Titus 3:3).

On the other hand, Paul insists that it is precisely those who have *abandoned* the faith who "forbid people to marry and order them to abstain from certain foods, which God created to be received with thanksgiving by those who believe and who know the truth." Paul explains, "Everything God created is good, and nothing is to be rejected if it is received with thanksgiving, because it is consecrated by the word of God and prayer" (1 Tim. 4:1, 3–5).

This admonition obviously reflects Jesus' attitude. In order to spare a family embarrassment and to keep their wedding celebration rolling, he turned water into the best of wine—thereby revealing his glory as the only begotten Son of the Father, giver of every good and perfect gift (see James 1:17).

Scripture's message, then, is that while pleasure itself is anything but wrong, unbridled pleasure-seeking is one sign of an ungodly life.

Warnings about hedonism have been numerous in non-biblical literature as well. Plato likened both pleasures and pains to the most powerful of detergents, for they can wash out even our dyed-in-the-wool convictions and inclinations to do what is right. He characterized what the Greeks called *sophrosyne*, or moderation, as an excellence or strength of human character. Once developed, this virtue enables us to continue to believe and do what is good and right in spite of the lures of pleasure and the dissuasions of pain. The emphasis must be on sticking with a worthwhile task in the face of hard work, weariness, boredom, or pain as much as on adhering to what is right when what is wrong offers more pleasure.

For the prospects of pain and its kin can compromise us as effectively as promises of pleasure. Sometimes, Plato thought, doing the right thing is a matter of sheer self-discipline and self-control, for we may find ourselves still *wanting* more pleasure and less pain than we should have, even if we then grind our teeth and manage to control the urges to indulge and pamper ourselves. True moderation, however, is a matter of coming to want only what is truly good or right. Truly moderate people, Plato believed, will not even want what they should not have.

> *Scripture's message, then, is that while pleasure itself is anything but wrong, unbridled pleasure-seeking is one sign of an ungodly life.*

Obviously, true moderation is better than mere self-control, for adherence to moderation makes it easier for us to do what we should do. Yet even if we can just barely control ourselves, it is clearly to our benefit, Plato concluded. He thus inaugurated the tradition of considering moderation one of the four "cardinal virtues." Along with wisdom, courage, and justice, moderation is a character trait we must develop if we are to lead happy, successful, and satisfying lives. Such strengths, or excellences of human character, as C. S. Lewis remarked, came to be called the cardinal virtues by both pagans and Christians because they considered them to be pivotal to living a genuinely human life.

The writers of Scripture would not quarrel with this belief. Recalling the lawless pleasure-seeking of the Sodomites, the apostle Peter likens some of the false, pleasure-bent prophets of his own day to brute beasts and creatures driven by instinct, fit "only to be caught and destroyed" (2 Peter 2:12b). The first chapter of Joshua is punctuated by God's commanding Joshua to be "strong and courageous" so that he can lead the Israelites into the Promised Land. Proverbs, among other biblical books, recommends and celebrates the sort of skillful living that constitutes wisdom.

We discipline ourselves because in heart-felt gratitude we no longer want to please ourselves but only to please God.

Biblical and nonbiblical writers, however, do not see entirely eye to eye about what comprises each of these virtues. Although Paul used the same Greek word for self-control in his list of the fruits of the Spirit that Plato used in the *Republic*, we must be cautious about declaring that Paul and Plato were referring to exactly the same thing. For Paul, self-control meant something that we need to exercise with regard to more than just the lures of hedonism.

Because those who belong to Christ Jesus "have crucified the sinful nature with its passions and desires" and now "live by the Spirit," they need to "keep in step with the Spirit" by controlling their hatred, jealousy, rage, selfish ambition, and envy, as well as by not succumbing to wrongful pleasures like sexual immorality and drunkenness (Gal. 5:19ff.).

In Christ, God has made us new creatures. But we still must work at putting to death our old, sinful natures and putting on our new, sanctified natures, "created to be like God in true righteousness and holiness" (Eph. 4:23f.; see also Col. 3:5–14 and Rom. 8:1–17). Exercising self-control is one way we put on new natures. Indeed, becoming self-controlled is essential to developing the sort of loving nature that is a hallmark of God's children, according to the testimony of the whole New Testament.

We discipline ourselves in these ways not so much because we merely want to be happy, successful, and satisfied, but because in heart-felt gratitude for what our Father has done for us, we no longer want to please ourselves but only to please God. In fact, this gratitude-prompted discipline is itself a sign that we have been born again as children of God. And as we try to discipline ourselves, we find that God himself, over time and through the sanctifying influence of the Holy Spirit, changes our personalities and moderates our passions in ways that allow us to please him and to become more conformed to the image of his Son.

12

The Lonely Path of Selflessness

Vinoy Laughner

> To the man who pleases him, God gives wisdom, knowledge and happiness, but to the sinner he gives the task of gathering and storing up wealth to hand it over to the one who pleases God.
>
> Ecclesiastes 2:26a

Someone once told me that living the Christian life is like living upside down: Everything that the world says is most important isn't. That statement is a generalization, of course, but when it comes to the central issues of our faith, it's very true. Being a Christian is a radical calling—a calling to despise and reject the values of this world and to be at odds with it.

What kind of inverted philosophy of life would teach that attaining real life comes through losing it? *Everyone knows that what constitutes success in life is "getting there" and being on top.*

What kind of backward people would champion the belief that the goals most people work themselves to the bone for are meaningless in themselves—even worse, a hindrance to following God? *Sour grapes! Whether you like it or not, money buys happiness and makes the world go 'round.*

> *The world's rewards are immediate, and we don't like to wait. Those who wait get second best. Though we know in our heads that this world is not our home, we've not been taught to develop the hearts of pilgrims.*

What kind of life worth living would take its cue from a leader whose greatest "success" was what any sane person would recognize as a failure and embarrassment? *Successful people model themselves after other successful people—winners. Haven't you heard the song "Hitch Your Wagon to a Star"?*

The world cannot accept who Jesus was, how he lived, and what he did, because in all he did he was selfless. To the world around him, he became a great fool. He did not live for personal success, comfort, a quality lifestyle, academic achievement, money, and self-betterment, or for hanging with the right crowd, social respect, coming in first and being on top. Instead, he denied himself his rights (Phil. 2:6–7), took the lonely, tortuous road of suffering, and spent himself for others. He laid down his life to please his Father and to save us.

Believers have been granted the privilege of not only believing on him—the part we love to talk about—but also of *suffer-*

ing for him—the part we shrink from, especially if it means deprivation of happiness in this world. Strangely, that's exactly what it might mean for us today in our consumer society.

The Bible plainly admonishes Christians not to love this selfish world, which *hates* God. But we too often find the world irresistible. For most of my life in Christ, I have heard clever and intelligent but erroneous explanations of how we can have the world and hate it too. The world's rewards are immediate, and we don't like to wait. Those who wait get second best. Though we know in our heads that this world is not our home, we've not been taught to develop the hearts of pilgrims; we keep searching for a heavenly refuge here, now—a little slice of heaven on this earth—and for a self-discovered, personally subsidized, secret passage back to the Garden. That is diabolical.

What Jesus stands for—genuine sacrifice, selflessness—the world hates. And because even as Christians we are at war with our old natures, we too rebel against Jesus' example. In this Vanity Fair culture the call to selflessness, unfortunately, makes even believers mighty uncomfortable. We've done a pitiful job of resisting the mold the world fashions for us.

The church in our culture is in the midst of an identity crisis: Are we lovers or haters of this world? We usually side with the world, I fear. Achieving the American Dream has come to be considered a worthwhile goal. To question that goal brings sideward glances of suspicion, even from the faithful.

Self-denial is *not* the American way. We've been taught that the better way is achieving a success that pulls others along and upward with us. God's promise that he will show his strength in our weakness baffles us. Nevertheless, when we are down to one penny, he will give us the faith to drop it into the offering plate, and he'll use it to fund world missions.

Whatever today's church exhibits to the culture, it's not selflessness. Sacrifice has become a feel-good-about-yourself option for those who can afford it. We give from our positions of security. Jesus' remark to the rich young ruler and his statement about the widow's penny, however, call for a humiliation we cannot bear. It's not an exaggeration to say that humility, self-sacrifice, negation of self, placing others first, and willingly taking a second or lower place are now like unappealing museum exhibits in a small, darkened room.

> *The essence of Jesus' life, service, death, and current ministry is selflessness. We've wanted to share in his power but not in his pain.*

The wise Teacher in Ecclesiastes teaches that wealth hoarded to the destruction of its owner is vanity, or meaninglessness. Here is a book for today. The security we spend our "meaningless" lives securing can be swept away in a moment.

I wonder whether Jesus had the aforementioned verse in mind when he told the story of the rich fool (Luke 12:16–21). (I have been awed by how much of the teaching and language of Ecclesiastes surfaces in our Lord's teaching; he must have loved the book.) A life lived for selfish security (and the rich man may even have been planning ahead not for himself but for his family) brings Jesus' rebuke of "fool" and the admonition to store real treasure in heaven. I am convinced that storing treasure in heaven comes not through our skill at ministry, our competence at leadership, or our records of pious achievements for the Lord; rather, it comes through what the world calls downright foolishness, through something we Christians don't fully understand—selfless sacrifice, perhaps unrewarded in this life, almost certainly humiliating and painful, but added to our accounts at the bank where things really count.

I have painted a distasteful picture. But I believe that self-lessness is about denial and pain. By its nature selflessness is discomforting. We've gambled for decades on a compromise, and we've been amassing fool's gold. We underestimate the hideous nature and power of sin. The essence of Jesus' life, service, death, and current ministry is selflessness. We've wanted to share in his power but not in his pain.

Learning to be selfless demands a faith that can bear humiliation and see beyond the rewards of this life. It might mean giving away what we've spent our lives protecting. While it might not be related to money (though it probably is, given Jesus' choice of examples), the Lord's call to deny ourselves security from anything but God alone is radical, painful, and uncomfortable, at best, but it is essential to true faith.

The world spends itself in vain attempts to graft meaning onto things that without God are meaningless, and races head-long toward selfish ambitions. The path is wide and it leads to hell.

Lord, give us the grace to fear you and obey your commandments, to follow your Son, our selfless Savior, who, while we were yet sinners, gave himself for us.

13

Rest for the Soul

Donald S. Whitney

All things are wearisome, more than one can say. The eye never has enough of seeing, nor the ear its fill of hearing.

Ecclesiastes 1:8

Karoshi is a Japanese word meaning "death from overwork." The syndrome is now so common in Japan that it claims as many as thirty thousand victims each year.

There's also a worldwide syndrome of "overwork of the soul." It afflicts everyone who has not accepted Jesus' offer in Matthew 11:28–30: "Come to me, all you who are weary and burdened, and I will give you rest."

Are You Soul-Weary?

When Jesus invited "the weary and burdened" to come to him, he was speaking primarily of weariness of the soul. What makes the soul weary? Our sin, its consequences, and the impact we feel from the sin of others. Additional factors include grief and sorrow, responsibility, conflict with others, and even physical weariness.

> *"Come to me, all you who are weary and burdened, and I will give you rest."*

Ecclesiastes is the classic description of humankind's frustrating search for soul-rest "under the sun"—instead of in the One who is above the sun.

In Ecclesiastes 1:13–15 the writer seeks to explore things in the past but concludes that "what is twisted cannot be straightened, what is lacking cannot be counted." Similarly, today some people seek individual or group therapy to explore things in their past in hopes of *correction*. Despite all the help they may get, they discover that they can neither change the past nor find rest for their souls.

Notice in the chart below how many of the ways people seek soul-rest are mentioned in Ecclesiastes and what each promises. Most of these pursuits offer something legitimate, but none can give soul-rest. Each promises "real fulfillment" if we get more of it than we have now. But there is no soul-rest because we never get enough to fulfill us.

Jesus Offers Soul-Rest

Soul-rest can never be found in anything under the sun. It can be found only by coming to a person, a person who came to us from above the sun—Christ Jesus. We must come to him first, not to baptism, the Lord's Supper, or the church, for they cannot give us rest. As Charles Spurgeon put it, "The soul is insatiable till it finds the Savior."

Ways People Seek Soul-Rest
and What Each Promises

Seeking soul-rest	Promise	Ecclesiastes
Individual or group counseling	Correction	1:13–15
Education or self-help	Transformation	1:16–18
Entertainment	Diversion	2:1–2
Alcohol and drugs	Stimulation	2:3
Work	Contribution	2:4–6
Buying, possessing, collecting	Satisfaction	2:4–8
Sex	Gratification	2:8b
Greatness	Recognition	2:9
Religion	Elevation	3:11

Jesus invites all who are weary and burdened in soul to come to him, regardless of their age, morality, education, social background, church experience, and the like. But we must come for ourselves. No parent, friend, or pastor can come for us. And we must forsake all other ways of finding soul-rest. Our souls cannot find rest by running between two masters.

How do we come to Jesus for this soul-rest? We come to him with our souls. Through prayer we approach him and open our weary and burdened souls to him. Then he enters. And there is rest, rest for our souls.

When Christ gives us soul-rest, there is rest for our consciences because he removes our sin-caused guilt. His soul-rest also includes rest for our minds, because he reveals himself as the truth of God. He ministers rest for our hearts, since we no longer have to search frantically for a haven of rest. In him there is rest from our fears, since our souls are in his loving, omnipotent hands for all eternity. Christ also provides rest regarding our sense of purpose, now that we have him to worship, love, and serve.

Christ Has Done the Work

Jesus has done all the work of paying for our sins. Just before his death on the cross he said, "It is finished!" Full payment for sin has been made. No payments have been needed for two thousand years. No further payment can be made or accepted.

Jesus has done all the work of making our peace with God. The apostle Paul declares, "Therefore, since we have been justified through faith, we have peace with God through our Lord Jesus Christ" (Rom. 5:1). Because of Christ, there is no more peace to be gained.

Even with all our obedience to God, our devotional habits, and our Christian deeds, we believers have no more forgiveness, no more peace, and no more credit for fulfilling God's requirements of righteousness than when we first believed. We have been delivered from spiritual *karoshi*. Let us rest in Jesus' payment, rest in his peace, rest in his fulfillment. Let us rest in the work of the only One who gives soul-rest.

14

A Desire to Please

Mike Malone

Now all has been heard; here is the conclusion of the matter: Fear God and keep his commandments, for this is the whole duty of man.

Ecclesiastes 12:13

Most pastors I know have experienced a rite of passage called "youth ministry." Working with young people is exhilarating, but it taxes creative and intellectual abilities to the fullest extent. Youth pastors must wrestle with the vital issues confronting their students, such as human sexuality. How far is too far? is the first question kids ask. I hear in their question something terribly troubling. What they actually are asking is this: What can I get away with? How promiscuous will God allow me to be?

Many students ask this question with sincerity. However, the question is framed with reference to them and not with reference to God: How much can I enjoy myself before God is upset enough to intervene? Rather, the question ought to be this: What will please God? What will give *him* great joy and delight?

> *The experience of the limitless love and grace of God makes disobedience a distressing consideration.*

The writer of Ecclesiastes experienced everything that anyone could desire. He got away with it all. Yet when in a position to weigh his life, he had two admonitions: "Fear God and keep his commandments, for this is the whole duty of man" (12:13b). The rest is vanity, emptiness, a vapor.

The fear of the Lord and obedience are not unrelated. Indeed, only the fear of the Lord compels a person to reshape the question to reflect a desire to please rather than a desire to indulge. Furthermore, only the fear of the Lord is sufficient to enable anyone to keep God's commandments with increasing faithfulness and for a lifetime.

For the Christian this fear is not laden with the weight of foreboding or gloom. It does not contain connotations of terror and dread. The presence of guilt produces terror and dread. For the Christian, guilt as a penal and legal matter has been addressed at the cross. The fear of the Lord is a bit different. It does not diminish the utter holiness of God nor the absolute character of his demands. In this fear another element is found: a horror that the One who has been so unimaginably merciful might be displeased. It is not less than regard for God; it is more. The experience of the limitless love and grace of God makes disobedience a distressing consideration. How often does it enter our minds that an action may offend the lover of our souls? Only the apprehension of the majesty of God wed to a sense of God's grace toward us is strong enough to transform us from people who evade God's commandments into people who desire to know and keep them, and delight in doing so.

Something of this reality is captured in Kenneth Grahame's *The Wind in the Willows*. Two characters, Mole and Rat, experience what can only be described as an encounter with the transcendent. Grahame's tale aptly illustrates what the fear of the Lord is for believers:

> Then suddenly the Mole felt a great awe fall upon him, an awe that turned his muscles to water, bowed his head and rooted his feet to the ground. It was no panic terror—indeed he felt wonderfully at peace and happy—but it was an awe that smote and held him and, without seeing, he knew it could only mean that some august Presence was very, very near. . . .
>
> Perhaps he would never have dared to raise his eyes, but that, though the piping was now hushed, the call and the summons still seemed dominant and imperious. . . . Trembling, he obeyed, and raised his humble head; and then, in that utter clearness of imminent Dawn, . . . he looked into the very eyes of his Friend and Helper. . . .
>
> "Rat!" he found breath to whisper, shaking. "Are you afraid?"
>
> "Afraid?" murmured the Rat, his eyes shining with unutterable love. "Afraid! Of Him? Oh, never, never! And yet—and yet—Oh, Mole, I am afraid."
>
> Then the two animals, crouching to the earth, bowed their heads and did worship.

The Bible promises that God will reward those who diligently seek him. That quest will result in the fear of the Lord. Steadfast obedience has one wellspring: this fear of the Lord, which is both the beginning of knowledge and the beginning of faithful living.

15

The Good News and the Good Life

Ken Myers

> Who is like the wise man? Who knows the explanation of things? Wisdom brightens a man's face and changes its hard appearance.
>
> Ecclesiastes 8:1

Thomas Merton once mused about people who prefer the secretion of clichés to thinking. Slogans are often a sign of the death of thought. Christian slogans, especially the kind that show up on bumper stickers, are no exception. What sort of communication is anticipated by the person who displays such slogans? My bumper having been a "stickee," I have a hunch that these pithy sayings are badges more for the benefit of the "wearer" than for the observer. But do they communicate anything beyond the identity of the driver?

Philosopher and historian Eric Voegelin, who wrote about many things (but not, I believe, about bumper stickers), once observed, "The answer will not help the man who has lost the question; and the predicament of the present age is characterized by the loss of the question rather than of the answer." The task of modern apologetics—which ought to inform the selection of bumper stickers—is to recognize how far from asking the basic questions about life modern culture has brought us.

In earlier ages the Big Questions were not as obscured. Even pre-Christian, classical ethics affirmed absolute principles of goodness and truth. Ethics as formulated by the Greeks answered the question, How do I live the good life?

That phrase "the good life" is probably the best antonym we have for *vanity,* the word used in Ecclesiastes to signify emptiness and stultifying boredom. The good life, in its best sense, is a life aligned with, suffused with, guided by, and animated by the Good. And, of course, there is only One who is Good.

Today the loss of the question is evident in the fact that "the good life" has become a slogan of consumption rather than a goal of moral discipline. In fact, the good life as conceived of by Madison Avenue looks suspiciously like the vanity that the Teacher in Ecclesiastes laments.

There is a great groundswell against the materialistic and hedonistic view of the good life, but much of it suffers from the shallowness of legalism. People declare that the nation suffers from the loss of traditional values. But when articulated, these values are often a list of rules, a set of standards for decent behavior. That sort of view of the good life is almost as limited as that of the "Miller Time" school.

For the gospel insists that the real question of the good life is a matter not of behavior but of the condition of the soul. Externalities, whether sybaritic activities and accessories or upright and impeccable behavior and demeanor, are always potentially counterfeit. When those who cry "Lord, Lord" are peremptorily dismissed from the presence of God, in whose name they have affirmed traditional values, perhaps they will realize that keeping the rules is essential to the good life but, by biblical standards, is never sufficient.

> *"The good life" has become a slogan of consumption rather than a goal of moral discipline.*

This awareness of the spiritual nature of goodness seems so basic as to be unforgettable. But the most basic things are often the easiest to mislay. Aspects of our amnesic modern culture make it increasingly easy to focus on what has been called "external conformity" to the law of God while forgetting the necessity of receiving and cultivating inner virtue.

Television—the medium in which we seem to live, move, and have our being—is much better at displaying external realities than at leading us to consider the complexities of internal realities. It thus tends to prejudice viewers in favor of movement over contemplation, becoming over being, and actions over motivations. It is better at exposing than at exploring.

Sociologist Joshua Meyrowitz, in his book *No Sense of Place*, has observed that TV encourages us to "focus on people who make one grand gesture or who complete a single courageous act that cannot be undermined by scrutiny. Our new heroes are men and women like Lenny Skutnik, who dove into the water—before television cameras—to save an airplane crash survivor, or Reginald Andrews, who saved a blind man's life by pulling him from beneath a New York subway car. . . . We can admire such isolated heroic acts; the pasts and the futures of such heroes remain comfortably irrelevant and invisible."

Keeping the rules is essential to the good life but, by biblical standards, is never sufficient. The good life is really more being than doing.

The modern heroic act, made accessible through television, is thus dislocated from character, from the biography of the hero. So the typical TV hero is not a model for the cultivation of virtue and the inner life (which might or might not result in heroic acts), or for the ordering of one's life around standards and principles that define what a good life is. Television heroes best demonstrate how heroes act, not how they think or meditate or pray.

The good life is really more *being* than doing. It is being that issues in doing, but it begins by the purification of the soul and continues in the cultivation, or sanctification, of the soul. Any answer to the probing search of Ecclesiastes that ignores the essentially spiritual nature of the good life will simply lead to another form of vanity.

For Reflection and Discussion

Chapter 1 **Vanity of Vanities, All Is Vanity**

1. How do nihilism, theism, and naive humanism express themselves in practice in contemporary culture?

2. On a scale from one to ten, with nihilism at number one and full-orbed theism at number ten, where would you rank our culture? What needs to be done to move that number closer to ten?

3. How can a Christian persuade a neighbor who is struggling with the apparent meaninglessness of life that life indeed has meaning?

4. What does Ephesians 1:3–14 teach about the meaning of life?

5. Why is it so difficult for humans who live as if there is no God to admit that God exists and has a purpose for them?

Chapter 2 **Wisdom under the Sun**

1. Modern society provides abundant opportunities to enhance one's knowledge: reading a book, taking a college class, cruising the Internet. But how does one go about gaining wisdom, especially divine wisdom?

2. Anderson claims that knowledge without wisdom breeds skepticism and cynicism. If that is true, what does knowledge coupled with wisdom produce?

3. Practically speaking, how does a life based upon the "wisdom of the world" differ from a life based upon "the fear of the Lord"?

4. The Teacher claims that knowledge in and of itself brings sorrow. In what ways are modern, secular universities, which have rejected Christianity as a unifying principle, depressing places?

5. We Christians maintain that truth is found in Jesus Christ. How does the search for truth continue once a person becomes a Christian?

Chapter 3 **Too Much Pleasure**

1. Do you agree with Henderson's assertion that "the sentimentalities of much modern 'worship'" stem from the search for pleasure?

2. The Teacher claims that pleasures are fleeting and ultimately do not satisfy. In what kinds of experiences have you personally discovered this to be true?

3. The line between appropriate enjoyment of God's gifts and making pleasure an idol is not always clear. What warning signals would alert you when you have crossed that line?

4. Henderson sees a relationship between the pursuit of sexual pleasure and abortion. What does this observation suggest is needed before the number of abortions can be significantly reduced in the United States?

5. The baby boom generation is frequently criticized for its pursuit of personal fulfillment. What does Matthew 16:24–26 teach about personal fulfillment?

Chapter 4 **The Vanity of Riches**

1. An old proverb instructs us to love people and use things. What drives humans to reverse the proverb, to love things and use people?

2. The search for perfection is a theme of this chapter. Why do so many Americans, including many Christians, have difficulty with jobs, marriages, and churches that are less than perfect?

3. Muether refers to Robert Bellah's observation that modern society has preempted the concept of a calling with the concept of a career. How can we recover the older, Reformation concept today? What are the marks of an individual who pursues a calling?

4. What does Matthew 19:16–24 say about Americans who are either wealthy or at least desire to be wealthy?

5. To what degree is modern evangelicalism, especially its megachurches and parachurch empires, driven by consumerism? How can the impulse that enthrones choice be tempered?

Chapter 5   **Thou Art the Man**

1. King David represents the very best of humankind and the very worst. What does this realism about the human condition say about the human tendency to seek out heroes and "strong" leaders, even in religious communities?

2. Do you agree with Sproul's contention that Michelangelo's sculpture of David is an ode to vanity? If Michelangelo were to take his cues from Sproul, how would the sculpture be different?

3. Notice Nathan's strategy in confronting David in 2 Samuel 12:1–6. Why are indirect strategies often more effective when confronting sin?

4. The psalmist declares that the sacrifices of God are a contrite heart and a broken spirit. How do a contrite heart and a broken spirit express themselves outwardly?

5. How do we keep in mind the folly of our labor?

Chapter 6   **Toiling the Soul**

1. Why is it so hard for humans to take responsibility for their problems, to admit, "I am the problem"?

2. Do you agree with Matzat that psychology and the counseling profession are largely out of step with biblical teaching? How would the profession be different if it began with the biblical diagnosis that sin is responsible for the human condition?

3. The first imperative in the Book of Romans is found in chapter 6, verse 11. Does this verse suggest that self-esteem has a place in the Christian life?

4. In what practical ways do the Scriptures instruct us to "get off ourselves and live in the benefits that belong to us in Christ Jesus"?

5. If the desire to preserve oneself and refuse to accept blame is as strong as the desire for food and shelter, how can we Christians hold that drive in check?

Chapter 7   **Fear God and Obey**

1. Information and knowledge are commodities that can be easily measured. Wisdom, on the other hand, is far more difficult to assess. How then can we gauge when we have gained in wisdom? What kinds of tests can we take to demonstrate that we have wisdom?

2. Malone implies that there are many intelligent fools. What public figures in the twentieth century might fit this description?

3. Why do most of us seek knowledge with greater intensity than we seek wisdom?

4. When have you reaped tragedy because you failed to apply rightly what you know?

5. If wisdom involves the ability to discriminate, how can we Christians develop the ability to discriminate?

Chapter 8   **And Then We Die?**

1. How can the gospel be communicated to postmodern individuals who celebrate, rather than lament, the apparent meaninglessness of life?

2. In light of Augustine's observation "Thou hast formed us for Thyself, and our hearts are restless till they find rest in Thee," might the appeal of the postmodern, "Be happy" approach to life be short-lived?

3. If postmodernism is "tailored to harden hearts much more ruthlessly" than was the skepticism of an earlier era, what chal-

lenges and opportunities does this new intellectual movement pose for the Christian faith?

4. Do you agree with Myers that the structures of modern life reinforce the postmodern spirit? How?

Chapter 9   **Vanity Overwhelmed by Purpose**

1. Sproul talks about proximate, remote, and ultimate purposes or goals. Have you ever adopted goals in life using these three categories? If not, give it a try.

2. The biblical story of Joseph illustrates how God's remote purposes can be served by people's proximate and contradictory purposes. In what past experiences was God overriding your goals and purposes with his own?

3. In the face of tragedy or crisis, how can we Christians cling to the truth that God's purposes, intentions, and will are always good?

4. Do you see a distinction, as do some Christians, between God's permitting things to happen and God's willing things to happen? If so, does God willingly or unwillingly permit things to happen? What is Sproul's position on the subject?

5. Why would God be less than God if he could not prevent certain things from happening?

Chapter 10   **Revelation above and below the Sun**

1. Do you agree with Coe that evangelicalism, in its zeal to defend the Bible, has disregarded other forms of revelation? What have been the consequences of that reductionism?

2. Coe claims that "only when *all* forms of revelation are taken together can we speak of the sufficiency of revelation." Based on this premise, how should science be used in the interpretation of the Bible?

3. What is the significance of propositional revelation? The Bible does not speak on every subject. So what is its primary goal and focus?

4. Why is propositional revelation by itself inadequate to save sinners?

5. Neoorthodoxy has a tendency to elevate the Living Word (Christ) at the expense of the Written Word (the Bible). Based on this chapter, identify the fallacy of this influential school of theology, and define the proper relationship between the two Words.

Chapter 11   **Enjoying God's Gifts**

1. Which of God's good gifts have his children not received with thanksgiving? Which of them have they scorned?

2. Why is moderation a more highly valued trait than self-control?

3. All humans, Christian or not, are capable of developing the four "cardinal virtues" of wisdom, courage, justice, and moderation. To what extent do we Christians have a "lower handicap" when it comes to developing these virtues?

4. What advice does the apostle Paul give in 1 Corinthians 8:9–13 concerning dealing with believers who may have scruples about some of God's good gifts?

5. Would your neighbor say that you have heeded the Teacher's advice, that you have accepted your lot in life and have found happiness in your work? If not, what must you do to find contentment?

Chapter 12   **The Lonely Path of Selflessness**

1. In what ways does the evangelical church promote selfishness over selflessness? How does evangelism sometimes reflect the same problem?

2. If the church does not exhibit selflessness to our society today, what traits does it exhibit?

3. Do you agree with Laughner that many Christians in the United States have confused the Christian life with the American Dream? What are the causes of that misidentification?

4. Identify a personal weakness that God has used (or can use) to demonstrate his strength.

5. Do you agree with Laughner that we want to share in Christ's power but not in his pain? In what ways might you be willing to share in his pain?

Chapter 13 **Rest for the Soul**

1. How might the fourth commandment help us to better appreciate rest from God?

2. According to John 20:31 and 2 Timothy 3:14–17, what is the role of Scripture in the sinner's finding rest in Jesus Christ?

3. What is the role of prayer in finding soul-rest?

4. Whitney states that "our souls cannot find rest by running between two masters." What other master tempts you not to look to Christ alone? What must you do to say no to that master?

5. When your soul is at rest in Christ, what outward and observable differences do others see in your life?

Chapter 14 **A Desire to Please**

1. What is the fear of the Lord?

2. Opinion polls claim that 98 percent of Americans believe in a god. Given the blatant disregard for keeping God's commandments in our society, what percentage of Americans would you say fear God?

3. How well do worship services in American churches lead worshipers to sense, as the Mole and the Rat did, the majesty of God, inspiring in them the fear of the Lord?

4. How can we Christians develop a fear of the Lord?

5. How can the church challenge individuals to take seriously the majesty of God and to fear him?

Chapter 15 **The Good News and the Good Life**

1. Myers contrasts the modern notion of the good life as consumption with the earlier notion of the good life as moral discipline. What is the exact relationship between the two, or to what degree is the former a parasite on the latter?

2. How does modern culture obstruct our willingness to raise the more important questions of life?

3. Myers claims that advocates of traditional values are more concerned with outward behavior than inner virtue. How would their rhetoric change if they heeded his concerns?

4. Do you agree that the very nature of television limits the medium's ability to grapple with the more serious issues of life, with character or inner virtue? What does this say about the limitations of Christian or religious television programming?

5. If we Christians turn our attention to developing inner character, does outward behavior then automatically take care of itself? How can we maintain a proper balance between the two concerns?